Thank you for your support during Helpful Phrases Launch Week!

To download the 12 printables included with the book, please visit the URL:

http://www.themilitarywifeandmom.com/helpful-phrases-printables/

Use the password: PHRASES12

Please note, the password is case sensitive and contains no spaces.

To download your free copy of Routines, Rhythms and Schedules, please visit the URL:

http://www.themilitarywifeandmom.com/routines-free

Use the coupon code LAUNCH30 at checkout

This code expires September 30, 2016 at 11:59 GMT and is only good for one use.

Helpful Phrases

How to Gain Cooperation From Toddlers and Preschoolers Without Lectures

By Rachel Normal and Lauren Tamm

Plus 10+ Free Printables With Phrases to Get You Started!

For our kids who make each day a unique parenting adventure.

For our spouses who support us each and every day.

For all the parents and caregivers who are looking to simplify parenting. You are among friends!

Contents

Introduction

Have the toddler and preschool years caught you by surprise?

We all come into motherhood unsure of what to expect. How will it feel to have a baby? How will I learn all the things I don't know? Soon, we find our footing with our bundles of joy. Feeding, cuddling, and changing diapers becomes part of our home landscape.

Babies are helpless and completely dependent upon us, and it's a beautiful season. Then the babies grow into pre-toddlers. These pre-toddlers begin crawling and communicating with grunts, sounds, and motions. They learn what areas in the home are off limits, and they begin to develop their own personalities.

Then they become toddlers...

They want to assert their own independence. They know exactly what they want: treats for breakfast, bedtime at 11:00 pm, and a mom who will immediately understand what they want at all times. They are fiery, exhilarating, precious, and at times, trying.

At this point we realize that having a peaceful home with toddlers isn't necessarily a given. We can be domineering, which can cause our toddlers to lash out further. We can give them whatever they want, which will create pint-sized tyrants. Or we can choose a better way: We can empower our children by creating healthy boundaries and routines that breed cooperation, predictability, and trust.

This is where *Helpful Phrases* comes in...

We wrote *Helpful Phrases* to give mothers a tool – one of many – to help parents communicate in a more effective way with their toddlers and preschoolers. While our little ones are like sponges, they are still limited in their ability to understand our messages.

Especially if we're long-winded...

This book will help you get to the heart of the matter and teach you how to communicate clearly with your toddlers and preschoolers. Not only will they feel security in knowing what you expect, you'll feel less frustrated as you throw off some previous forms of communication that haven't worked for you.

We hope you'll find great success as we have with using these helpful phrases to foster independence, cooperation, and a positive environment in your home.

Rachel, *A Mother Far from Home*

"The way we talk to our children becomes their inner voice."

Peggy O'Mara

Why Short Phrases?

My toddler was "in the zone." In that moment, I felt like a nuclear bomb could go off right next to us, and he wouldn't even notice. We were preparing to leave the house for my daughter's doctor appointment. My toddler came along because it never seems worth the money to pay a babysitter for a quick appointment.

After spending exactly 8.67 minutes in a serious debate over shoes, my toddler finally agreed to put on his crocs, and we left the house. The baby screamed the whole way to the appointment. It was only 9:36 am and already my head throbbed with each passing second. Deep breath. We pulled into the parking lot with exactly three minutes to spare.

We were going to make it! Right until my toddler lost his matchbox car. It dropped between the seats into an abyss of crumbs, broken toys, and spare change.

I told him, "It's okay. We'll get the car later. Right now we have to go inside."

He didn't listen to one word I said. My toddler was on a mission to find a matchbox car, and he wasn't going to give up until he found it. Like I said, a nuclear bomb could go off right next to us, and in that moment, he wouldn't even notice.

Now you might be thinking, Okay lady, take the bull by the horns here. Tell your toddler to forget about the stupid car, get a move on, and take him into the doctor's office already. I understand exactly where you are coming from—a place of logic. But let me explain why I didn't take that approach.

A Look Inside the Toddler and Preschooler Brain

I could spend hours rambling about the brain of toddlers and preschoolers and all the fancy science behind it. We could talk synapses, myelination, frontal cortex, neuron, cortical and subcortical structures, but truthfully, who has time for that?

Let's keep it simple. You need a basic understanding of how your child processes information. This is the key to unlocking better listening, cooperation, fewer power struggles, and more peaceful days. Knowing how your child's brain works empowers you to shift your approach to one that is more effective. Let's work smarter, not harder, right?

Important Structure #1: Prefrontal Cortex

This is your child's thinking brain, and it's located in the front of the brain, right behind the forehead. It handles logic, empathy, compassion, creativity, self-regulation, self-awareness, predicting, planning, problem-solving, and attention.

While the prefrontal cortex regulates behavior and impulsivity, it does not fully mature until we reach our mid-twenties. While an adult's prefrontal cortex is fully mature and operates at an extremely high level, it is the most immature part of your child's brain.

So when you are thinking, "Geeze, we really need to hurry and get to this appointment."

Your child is thinking, "Geeze, I love that matchbox car so much. If I could find it, that would make me happy and life would be grand."

This doesn't mean small children completely lack the ability to control impulsivity and to process logic, but their ability is limited. The thinking brain grows as your child grows, but when you struggle with behavior and listening, it's important to understand your child's limited development.

Now that we know about the immature prefrontal cortex (i.e. the logical brain), it is easier to understand why getting your child to put on his shoes or stop looking for a

99 cent matchbox car hurts your brain more than a college calculus test.

Important Structure #2: Limbic System

This is your child's emotional brain. It processes memory, stress responses, nurturing, caring, separation anxiety, fear, rage, social bonding, and hormone control. During the early years, the limbic system is the front seat driver of the brain, and it doesn't care what anyone in the backseat has to say about it.

Toddlers and preschoolers react to the world in the form of feelings (sometimes gigantic ones), stemming from the limbic system in the front seat. Meanwhile, the prefrontal sits in the backseat (figuratively, not literally) trying to talk some sense into it, but the limbic system is in overdrive.

Let's say you're outside with your child, and he tries to drink the rainwater from a puddle on the ground. Using your prefrontal cortex (the logical part of your brain), you're thinking about him ingesting E.coli and a heinous GI virus. Then you think about him being up at 3 a.m. while he empties his dinner into the toilet. Logically, you'd rather avoid the consequences of your child ingesting E.coli, so you tell him to stop.

Except He Doesn't

He's thinking about how fun it is to drink water off the ground. He's thinking about how it makes him feel happy.

When you tell him to stop, he doesn't think, "Oh yeah, this grimy puddle is gross, and it could make me sick."

Right now, he isn't using the logical part of his brain. Instead, he thinks, "My mom doesn't want me to be happy. Rainwater makes me happy. Why won't she let me have what makes me happy?"

That's the difference between adults and small children. You are operating from the prefrontal cortex, which is fully developed and logical. Your child is operating from the limbic system, which is illogical and driven purely by emotion.

Important Structure #3: Synapses

Synapses are the connections inside your child's brain, and this is how the brain communicates. Think of them as a huge pile of tangled string all in one ball. Each string represents a communication pathway in your child's brain.

This is the most interesting part about synapses: when your child is born, his brain has nearly all the neurons (or string) it will ever have. Then between birth and age three, your child experiences the most dramatic brain growth spurt of his entire life.

Your child's brain is building connections, learning and growing, all in an effort to determine what is important information and what is not. By the time your child is three years old, his brain will reach 80 percent of its adult volume after building all these synapse connections.

After the age of three, the synapses that go unused start to fizzle. The ones that are used grow stronger. By the time your child reaches adulthood, 50 percent of the synapses will fizzle out. This is all part of normal brain development.

The important relationship between synapses and how we communicate with kids is this:

When you are struggling with listening, communication or power struggles, remember synapses. Remember that your child's brain is experiencing the greatest growth spurt of its life. It's building and growing connections at a faster rate than he will experience at any other time in his life.

Repeated use strengthens a synapse. This is why consistent approaches to listening and behavior are so important. The groundwork you lay during the early years sets the foundation for the years to come. When you use the consistent approaches of short phrases, you will see those synapses strengthen and grow. Eventually, those synapses become so strong they'll guide your child towards better listening, and behavior gets easier and easier.

Why Short Phrases?

Your child's brain craves clear communication. You may find yourself in a situation when your child is melting down or determined to carry out a power struggle. You may ask your child a series of questions and he responds "No!" to everything you say.

Do you want to go to the bathroom? No!

Do you want to eat dinner? No!

Do you want to read a book? No!

Do you want to play with blocks? No!

As a parent or caregiver, this is a very frustrating situation, but kids do this for a reason. Starting at about 18 months, your child begins to understand that he is a separate person from you and others. He also understands that his own thoughts and feelings are separate from yours. And he understands that you may not share the same viewpoint.

This is where the boundary testing begins. These are intense moments between a young child and a parent.

Enter Helpful Phrases

Using quick, clear bursts of communication with your child is more important than ever. Your child is desperate to feel understood, desperate to feel comfortable with his place in the world, and desperate to understand what you are truly asking of him.

Many times, your kids may not even understand what you are instructing them to do. So what do they do? They guess. Or they ignore you completely. When they guess wrong or ignore you, you get crabby, tired, and irritable. Power struggles become the norm, and your day-to-day life with kids feels more like circling the drain rather than thriving and enjoying your days.

Throughout this book, we will show you how to use short, simple phrases to gain cooperation, encourage better listening, and minimize power struggles.

The Best Part?

We are going to empower you with phrases that will help you respond to your child when you are faced with a variety of challenging parenting scenarios. When your child won't listen you, when your child refuses to participate in age-appropriate chores, when your child is picky at the dinner table, or when your child fights bedtime. These are just a few examples of the powerful ways phrases can shape your parenting into easier, more relaxing days.

You are at a window of opportunity. Positive and effective techniques discussed in the coming chapters will empower you as a parent or caregiver to teach your child to listen, comprehend, and if you play your phrases right, put on his shoes and help you get to appointments on time.

"Respecting children teaches them that even the smallest, most powerless, most vulnerable person deserves respect."

L.R. Knost

How to Get Started Using Short Phrases

While our short and helpful phrases will work wonders for your home, they must start with a good foundation. What's in a good foundation?

If your kids don't know what you expect, don't know their boundaries, and never know what will happen next, that's a lack of foundation.

Let's dig into creating a good one.

Managing Expectations

While it may seem that an obedient child is obedient 100 percent of the time, that is impossible! Even adults don't do what they want to do 100 percent of the time. Babies are born curious, and they will continue to show their curiosity in ways that manifest as disobedience as they grow and develop.

The goal isn't to have a child who does what you ask every single time but to grow a child who respects your word and learns to make good decisions on their own.

Maintaining Healthy Sleep Habits

While this book isn't about sleep, per se, we'd be remiss if we didn't mention the importance of rest on our children (and our own) behavior. Children who are well-rested are calmer, more content, and better able to follow instructions without becoming overwhelmed.

At minimum, babies should take a few naps a day, toddlers at least one nap a day, and preschoolers should have a regular rest time if they've grown out of naps. At night, your children will be doing well to get between 10-12 hours of uninterrupted sleep. You might be thinking this is impossible, but we assure you it isn't.

By making changes to a few key habits, you can watch your baby or toddler transform from a tired one into a more content and peaceful child.

For more information and help with baby sleeping habits, check out:

For the Love of Sleep eBook by Lauren Tamm
http://www.themilitarywifeandmom.com/sleep

From Coos to Snooze eCourse by Rachel Norman
http://coostosnooze.com/

Self-Care for You

Mothers are naturally sacrificial and outward looking. They meet the needs of their family all day and night, and often neglect themselves because there are only a set number of hours in a day. While this can be necessary at times, it is not a habit that will serve moms well in the longer term.

When mothers lack sleep, time alone, and refreshment they become short-tempered, more prone to hormonal imbalances, and weary. Although it's great to persevere when you are feeling down, the goal is to manage your own needs in a way that helps you be a better mother to your children.

Here are some ideas for ways to take care of yourself well:

Make time for a daily shower or bath.

Put on "real" clothes. This doesn't have to be something fancy, but at least trade in pajamas for an outfit, even if it is yoga pants.

Get a low maintenance haircut so you can feel more put together daily.

Maintain friendships even if they look like playgroups, mom dates, or trips to the park with friends.

Take time alone. Whether it's a night or an entire weekend, make time alone to refresh a priority. Hire a sitter, ask a family member, trade nights with a friend, or beg a loved one to help!

Exercise. Often we feel too tired to exercise, but exercise itself gives energy! You can take the kids for a stroll around the neighborhood or even do a fitness DVD with the kids at home.

Drink water. Aside from the added benefit of weight loss that comes when drinking adequate water, water will help keep you hydrated and you'll feel better than you can imagine from this one simple step.

The Importance of Routine

There is no way to overstate the importance of a good routine for your babies, toddlers, and preschoolers. Not only do they sleep better and eat better, they behave better as well. Children are consistently bombarded with new things to see and learn and it can become over-stimulating quickly.

By having a good routine in place your children have the space and time to play freely and rest well. You don't have to schedule out your day minute by minute to have a good routine. Even with only a few elements of your day set in stone, you are still free to add in spontaneous fun.

Times of day best with a routine:

- Breakfast, lunch and dinner
- Snacks
- Naps
- Bedtime
- Structured playtime

Try creating a routine for your little ones and watch the difference it makes. (See Bonus Chapters 16 & 17 for more on playtime and routines.)

View our book with 30+ routines for babies ages 6 weeks to 5 years including printables here:

Routines, Rhythms and Schedules: How to Simplify Life With Kids

http://www.themilitarywifeandmom.com/routines-rhythms-schedules-book

Consistency

As it applies to most things in life, consistency in parenting is of great benefit to you and your children. When children know what to expect from you they will be more cooperative and less resistant to your instructions and ideas.

If you create family rules, routines, and traditions be sure to keep them. Whether you have to set alarms, use a timer, put things on the calendar, or hang reminders around the house, do whatever it takes to help keep you consistent.

Modeling Good Behavior and Listening

If we want our children to listen and respond to our instruction, we need to clearly show them what we expect. Children are not born knowing what we want from them. They don't know it's good to put away their dishes, whisper if a baby is asleep, or to not hit or bite. We need to be short, concise, and clear in our expectations.

Before we can expect our children to do something we must show them how. By modeling what we expect and being consistent in following up, our children will quickly begin to understand what we want.

What to Do When Using Short Phrases

While phrases will ultimately change how you communicate with your kids, there may be a few other factors you need to consider to encourage your toddlers and preschoolers to cooperate. Because children are naturally curious and will push the boundaries, we need to be sure they are paying attention before we give them instructions.

Make Eye Contact

When you ask your children to do (or stop doing) something in particular, make eye contact first. If they aren't looking at you, it's impossible to tell if they've heard you. Particularly if they are engaged in another activity, ask your children to look at you and be sure they're paying attention before you speak.

Get Down to their Level

With pre-toddlers and toddlers, the best thing you can do is get down at eye level. Whether you squat, sit, or hold them as you speak, being face to face will help them hear and understand you. This also helps them feel connected to and accepted by you.

Keep It Short

We all have a tendency to talk more than we need to with our kids. Short, clear phrases will get the point across, and the more you speak the more chance your children will get confused. Don't use a paragraph when a sentence will do.

When to Repeat

While children will need family rules, boundaries, and consequences repeated over the longer term, it is best to avoid repeating your instructions in the moment. If you've looked your child in the eye at their level and asked them to do something, don't repeat yourself over and over again. This communicates to your child you were not serious the first time.

Repeat the phrases throughout your days, weeks, and months, but don't repeat yourself in the moment unless you know your child hasn't understood. If they refuse to do what you've asked, then simply give your child the consequence for that particular behavior.

Setting the Foundation Is Key to Success

When you start using short phrases regularly, consistently, and with purpose, you'll see immediate results with your toddlers and preschoolers. Using phrases with a positive and kind attitude will help children feel heard, understood, and give you the cooperation you are seeking.

"What every young child would tell us, if they could, is to please hold onto them, not take their actions personally, and to love them despite their immaturity."

Dr. Deborah MacNamara

Behavior and Obedience

It all started out innocently enough. The kids were watching a bit of cartoons before we moved onto the next thing. All three little ones, lined up in a row with their eyes glued to the TV. I told them to turn it off once. I said it again. Crickets. I even called their names and received no response. Finally, I went and stood in front of the TV, got angry, and said, "You aren't listening!" then turned the TV off myself.

As you can imagine, this resulted in a crying, flopping rage from all three kids.

Since then, I've changed tack. While I still expect my children to listen and obey my instructions, I do it in a way they are able to understand, process, and respond to. I keep things simple, clear, and straightforward.

In order to gain cooperation from our children, we need to get down to their level, give them instructions they can understand, and give them the tools to cooperate.

Here are a few phrases that help encourage good behavior and obedience to your instructions.

"Let's try that again"

Instead of immediately imposing a consequence or punishment for your child's behavior, calmly take a second. If they acted impulsively but without malice, you may want to step back and give them a do-over.

"Can you think of a better way?"

Children aren't born knowing how to respond in any given situation. If you see they responded carelessly or hastily, instead of saying, "I don't like how you did that," try another way. This phrase will encourage them to think before acting again. Often, if we react strongly and negatively, they'll dig their heels in stubbornly. Remember, the goal is not to "win" but to come alongside our kids and teach them.

"Eyes"

This is a household favorite around here. When I need to give my children instructions to follow, I make sure they are looking at me so we're all making eye contact. I will say, "Eyes, kids" and wait until everyone is looking my way. When you're face to face, it's much more likely the child will hear, understand, and carry out your instructions.

"Yes, mommy"

This phrase encourages cooperation and ownership of your request. If you ask your child to help you carry out a chore, encourage them to agree with you by saying, "Yes, mommy." If you don't hear an immediate response, pause for a few moments and give them a chance to respond. Then offer guidance if needed. By acknowledging you with this phrase, the child acknowledges to you they will do this and they are far more likely to carry it out. If they hesitate to give the phrase, you can ask follow-up questions to be sure they understand.

"We are kind; we don't hit"

Toddlers and preschoolers often go through phases where their physical response to emotional overwhelm or frustration is hitting, kicking, or biting. Instead of giving a lengthy lecture about why these behaviors are unacceptable, short and sweet is the way to go.

"Use your words"

Children have strong emotions and are still learning to process and control their reactions. Instead of asking our children to stop crying or not throw a tantrum, give them an alternative. "Use your words" encourages children to calm down and think about what's bothering them. My son reacts strongly and quickly to many situations, and this phrase helps him to center himself and speak instead of cry on the floor.

"Repeat what mommy said"

One thing parents of small ones do a lot of is repeat. We repeat the same activities and phrases day after day. However, instead of saying your instruction five times and becoming background noise, encourage your children to recall what you've said by asking them, "Repeat what mommy said." This also helps them process and remember your request.

"Give me a minute"

We all have times when we feel overwhelmed and stressed during the day with our children. Instead of getting more and more worked up as the day goes on, teach your toddlers and preschoolers to give you a minute of peace. Whether you go to the bathroom, sit quietly with a cup of coffee, or go stand outside, teach your children that when you say, "Give me a minute, please," you are asking them to play independently until you return.

"Did you really mean that?"

When your child says something impulsively and out of character, give them a chance to do it over. If it isn't a consistent and persistent behavior, allow them to rephrase their backtalk by giving them grace to start again. Often, this opportunity is enough to soften their hearts and avoid a power struggle.

"Show mommy"

If your child is all talk and no action – or it feels that way – use this phrase to help spur them on. Instead of talking about a task, complaining, or whining, have them show you exactly what they are trying to say. Showing your kids that you're willing to listen goes a long way.

Turning off the TV takes practice

My toddlers or preschoolers may never be excited to turn off the TV, but we have a good routine now. I warn the kids that the TV will be turning off as soon as this show is over. A few minutes before, I'll say, "Eyes" and when they're all looking, I say, "What did mommy say?"

The response? No screaming, flailing, or whining. Just a chorus of, "We know, mommy!"

"My child is not giving me a hard time, my child is having a hard time."

Coping With Big Emotions

The transition to a new preschool presented big challenges: new environment, teachers, and kids. Plagued by intense separation anxiety, my son didn't quite know how to manage his big feelings. But it was time. Today he was starting a new preschool.

Reaching each arm through the sleeves of his shirt, he tried his hardest to get ready for school and be brave. I finished packing his lunch and even tried to give him something to look forward to by cutting out his sandwich in the shape of a dinosaur. But on the way to school, his emotions took over as he cried and cried in the backseat of the car. From the rearview mirror, I could see the tears streaming down his face.

"What's wrong, buddy?" I asked.

No response came, just a few more cries and whimpers. I felt so guilty sending him to a new school. I wanted to help him feel better, but I didn't know where to begin.

"Everything will be fine. Stop crying, okay?"

But he couldn't stop crying. He didn't know what he was feeling or how to deal with it.

Think about how you would respond if this scenario played out with your child. What phrases would you need to effectively help your child process emotions in a variety of situations? Is it possible to create a teachable moment and help your child navigate big feelings?

Here's What the Research Says

Initially when your child acts upset, angry, or anxious, your first gut reaction may be to say something like, "There's no reason to get upset." Or "It's not so bad." Or "Stop crying!"

Unfortunately, these phrases aren't helpful because they don't teach kids how to regulate or process emotion. Rather, these phrases dismiss your child's emotions, encouraging him to bottle up feelings. Later that day or week, your child may act out or meltdown without a clear or obvious source. This often leaves us feeling confused as parents, but here is what is happening: Your child is looking for a way to release emotion because they aren't yet equipped with coping skills to process emotion.

The Solution: Emotion Coaching Through Phrases

The best way to help kids process emotions is through emotion coaching, and in doing so, you are enabling your child to emotionally self-regulate now and in the future.

Teaching kids to self-regulate emotions is your most important job as a parent. And the research backs it up.

Kids with better self-regulation skills tend to have better life outcomes in the form of higher test scores and better behavior when parents talk to them about their feelings, show empathy, and explore constructive ways to cope.[1,2]

Phrases to Help Your Child Cope With Emotions

"I wish you a thousand..."

Using the word "thousand" helps kids visualize abundance and see something positive that they really want. When your child is upset about something, these statements also help kids to re-frame the idea into a better scenario.

Here are a few examples:

Child: "I don't want to move to a new home."
Parent: "I wish you a thousand friends at our new home."

Child: "I hate playing at this park."
Parent: "I wish you a thousand parks that are the most fun and coolest in the world."

---

[1] J Youth Adolesc. 2011 Apr; 40(4): 428–441.
[2] Developmental Psychology. 1991. 27(3): 448-445

"I wish you a thousand..." statements can encourage and help your child focus on something that would help them feel happy. They can pretend and fix the problem using imagination. "I wish you a thousand..." statements perfectly suit the brain development of younger children and use their greatest asset—the imagination—to solve a problem. Children ages 2-8 don't yet have the ability to fully distinguish what is impossible from what is unlikely to happen but could technically happen. Thus, using fantasy statements calms your child and helps them process stress. These statements allow your child to believe that, yes, they could (possibly) have a thousand friends when they move to a new home.

"Can you draw a picture of your feeling?"

Encourage your child to color, draw, or sculpt their feelings. You can alternatively ask, "What does your feeling look like?" Not all kids are able to put feelings into words, but they are usually able to draw something they envision in their mind. If you don't know what the picture is exactly, share a simple description such as, "I see two brown lines and lots of pink swirls. I wonder what it could be." If you are correct in your description, your child will carry on or maybe add more to the drawing. If you are wrong, he will surely correct you.

Your child may draw an angry, happy, sad, or excited face. They may scribble all over the paper. It may be something abstract. Or maybe it's a picture of the scenario that happened that day. For example, it may be a picture of two kids at the park. After your child gets it all down on paper, ask them to tell you about it. The picture is a great starting point to help you understand your child's emotion so you can help them process and move forward.

"Let's take a deep breath"

When a kid breaks down, they are telling you they are no longer able to cope. Because kids don't learn anything when they are in this disorganized state, teaching them how to calm or soothe themselves is helpful. Help your child learn how to make his belly move up and down by taking big breaths. Do it together, holding your hands over your bellies. Modeling the behavior helps get your child started.

"I would've felt {insert feeling: angry, upset, anxious, etc} if {insert cause} happened too"

Empathy is the foundation for helping kids feel both validated and heard, and it begins with the ability to see the world through the eyes of another person. Or to walk a mile in another's shoes. Telling your child that you would've felt the same way helps them feel that they are not alone. That you understand where they are coming from with their big and intense feelings. Knowing that you understand can start the calming cascade.

"I see you are {insert feeling: angry, upset, anxious, etc} about {insert cause}"

Describe to your child exactly what you see in the moment. For example:

"I see you are upset about leaving the park."
"I see you are angry about not getting to play with your favorite toy."

You don't have to be correct in guessing what your child is upset about. This is the perfect opportunity to allow them to correct you and share what they are truly upset about. Using this phrase is a great alternative to asking "What's wrong?" When you ask "What's wrong?" your child may get upset or not respond at all. When you use the phrase "I see you are…" this helps you name a feeling for your child. And if you are not correct in guessing, your child will likely let you know.

"Does your feeling have a name?"

When big feelings are raging out of control in your child's emotional brain, help your child name the feeling that's upsetting him. This helps your child tap into the logical part of the brain to make sense of his experience and feel more control. Your child may call his feeling sad or he may call his feeling "Doggie" or "Bob." Truly, it doesn't matter. After your child names the feeling, ask him to tell you what "sad" or "Doggie" or "Bob" does. Encourage him to describe the situation or the feeling. Research shows that merely assigning a name or label to what we feel literally calms down the activity of the synapses firing in the emotional brain.

"What do you wish someone would say to you?"

This is an excellent backdoor way to learn what your child secretly yearns for others to say to him or her. This question can help you learn what your child needs to feel better.

"If your friend felt {insert feeling: angry, upset, anxious, etc} about {insert cause}, what would you do to help them feel better?"

Sometimes kids are so upset that their brain enters fight or flight mode, and they simply cannot tap into the logical side of their brain and name the feeling. Ask them to imagine a friend in a similar situation. Paint the picture or scenario for them. For example: "A boy took Jacob's dinosaur puzzle. Jacob felt so sad and angry that he took his dinosaur puzzle. What would you do to help him feel better?" Allow your child the chance to respond. If they don't respond or they aren't sure what to say, ask, "Do you think a hug would help her feel better?" Or "Do you think offering to play with her would help?" Sometimes just walking your child through a hypothetical scenario allows them to process and work through the emotions.

"The last time we tried…"

If you discover a strategy that works well to help your child process emotion, remind your child of what worked well before. Walk them through the problem, the solution, and how their emotions shifted during a previous situation. For example, "The last time you felt upset about going to school, we took some deep breaths and you felt calmer. Do you remember the last time we tried deep breathing?" Allow your child a moment to process what you said, then ask, "Would you like to try taking a few deep breaths again?"

"You are safe. I am here with you."

No matter what emotion your child is struggling with, it is always comforting to know that mom or dad is there to provide a safe space. This phrase encourages kids to know they can share their emotions and feelings with you – no matter how illogical and emotionally driven they are – without judgment, shame, or punishment. Sometimes kids simply want a hug or a shoulder to lean on.

Processing Emotions Starts With Phrases

Over the process of several weeks, I started helping my son to process his separation anxiety with school. On the way to school each day, my son and I talked about the names of his feelings. We talked about what he would say to someone who was scared about going to school.

When he got home each day, we practiced putting our hands on our bellies and making them move up and down. I reminded him to "make his belly move" when he felt scared or sad at school. It wasn't long before my son was practically jumping out of the car each morning to run into school. He would high-five the kids and participate in all the school activities throughout the day.

Right now, you are building and growing your child's emotional regulation skills. Years down the road when your child feels anxious about buying a new house or starting a new job, these emotional regulation skills are going to help him process emotion and stress as well as help him make good life choices – even when life gets overwhelming.

"Childhood is a small window of time to learn and develop at a pace which is right for each individual child."

Magda Gerber

Raising a Great Listener

I was out of the room for only a second to grab his pajamas. As I closed his dresser drawer, I could hear him in the kitchen shouting, "I GOT IT." Teaching kids to listen feels like summiting Everest some days. When I walked back into the kitchen, my boy was stark naked, standing on the counter holding a glass of water.

My son was asserting his independence, climbing on the counter to get a glass from the cabinet, turning on the water, and grabbing a drink. He thought he was useful and helpful by doing something all by himself.

But immediately after seeing him, I yelled, "Get DOWN!"

He responded by giggling and continuing to grab another drink from the faucet. He was so excited with his accomplishment, he wanted to show me how he could do it again.

Now I was starting to get plain mad, "How many times have I told you? You're not allowed on the counter!"

It's hard not to laugh at the cuteness of a young boy standing on the counter, proud of his glass of water, naked and all. But when your child doesn't listen, you feel like you have a very defiant child on your hands.

Short Phrases That Encourage Great Listening

Often times it is not our boundaries and expectations that require adjustment. Rather, it is the way we communicate those boundaries and expectations with our words. Simply re-framing the idea or choice of words can result in better listening from your child.

"Would you like to {choice #1} or {choice #2}?"

Gaining cooperation from children starts with fulfilling their need to make choices and allowing them to be active participants in their own life. This does not equate to permissive parenting but rather engaged parenting where you strike a balance between choices and appropriate boundaries. Offering kids choices teaches them that they are loved, capable, and trustworthy and that they matter.

Here are a few examples of choices:

"Would you like the blue cup or the red cup?"
"Would you like to play with the train set or the dolls?"
"Would you like to play quietly with your toys or help mom cook dinner?"

"Show me how to _____"

You may find yourself stuck when you say things like, "Can you show me how to pick up the toys?" Your child may promptly answer with a resounding, "No!" And while offering directive statements does not eliminate outbursts of "No!" it can help minimize abrasive responses and power struggles.

Use "Show me how to _____" when you want your child to initiate a task such as picking up the toys, getting into the car seat, or brushing teeth. If you can model the behavior for your child while using the phrase, this helps get kids started. They will see the activity as a cooperative effort rather than being bossed around.

"What is a better way?"

Your initial reaction to behaviors like throwing, hitting, running, jumping, or emotional outbursts may be to say, "Stop that!" or "I told you no!" or "Don't throw the ball!" Using these phrases make us think and feel like we are teaching kids to listen, but accusatory statements often result in push-back rather than cooperation from kids.

I don't want to give the wrong idea. You will use the words "No," "Stop," and "Don't" while parenting. But the goal is to use them as sparingly as possible to make them incredibly effective when we do say those words.

When trying to guide your child towards better listening throughout the day, an excellent phrase to use is, "What is a better way?" This phrase is based on process criticism, and it allows your child to problem solve and use creativity to discover a better solution. Children who are approached with process criticism have better self-worth, mood, and persistence.

This is different from person criticism, which involves saying things like, "I'm disappointed in you." Or "You're naughty." Or "You don't listen." Person criticism directly attacks the child's character and they start to view themselves in a negative light. They start to think, "I'm bad."

Now you might be thinking, *What if my child ignores me or says, "Nothing is a better way"?* This is a perfect time to follow up with, "I remember the last time we tried to roll the ball. Show me how to roll the ball."

"I notice that _____"

This phrase helps parents make a statement of fact that describes the situation rather than accusing or criticizing. Simply share with your child exactly what you observe at the moment. If your child is jumping on the couch, you can say, "I notice you really like to jump!" Or if you ask your child to brush his teeth, and he continues to intently play with his blocks, you can say, "I notice that you aren't done playing with the blocks."

The goal is to validate what your child wants to do at that moment. To allow their feelings to be heard. Validating helps your child feel a sense of control and breeds more cooperation in the long run.

After sharing your observations with your child, go ahead and follow up with what you would like them to do instead. Many of the phrases in this chapter are excellent follow-up phrases.

Here is an example:

Your child is playing with toys, but it's time for him to go to bed. You say, "It's time for bed," to which he responds, "No!"

Share your observations: "I notice that you aren't done playing with your toys."

Follow up with something your child can do: "You can bring one quiet toy with you to bed." Or "You can play with your toy again tomorrow when you wake up."

You can also follow up with other phrases from this chapter: "Would you like to read a story in bed or go to bed right away?" Or "Show me how to put the toys away so we can use them right way again tomorrow." Or "When you put the toys away, then you can play with them right away in the morning." Or "What do you need to feel ready to go to bed?"

"When you _____, I feel _____ because _____"

Explaining how you feel helps kids understand your point of view. Describe exactly how you feel to your child. If you are working on empathy training, this is a great time to encourage your child to take your perspective. For example, "When you run away from mommy, I feel worried because a car could hurt you." Or "When you don't pick up the toys, I feel sad because there is no one to help mommy."

The goal is not to throw yourself a parenting pity party but rather to allow your child to learn and understand the emotions of others. To learn that their feelings are not the only feelings in play. Empathy is key to raising a child who listens well. The more your child learns to empathize with the feelings of others, the more likely he is to demonstrate a caring, understanding, and kind attitude towards others' wants, needs, and desires. Hence, when you ask your child to pick up the toys, he is motivated to complete the task because he understands where you are coming from. He understands your perspective too; not just his own.

"When you _____, then you _____"

Use a "when...then" phrase to offer your child an incentive for completing what you are asking. It reframes what you are asking to encourage the child to listen in order to gain something important to him.

Here's an example:

You tell your child to come inside for dinner, and he responds with, "One minute!" Or "NO!" Or ignores you altogether. You repeat yourself again and again until you and your child embattle into a power struggle followed by a meltdown. The "when you, then you" phrase is a simple way to approach a situation that would normally result in power struggles and yelling.

"When you finish cleaning up your toys, then you can continue watching your TV show."

"When you get dressed, then you can go outside and play with your friend."

"When you've brushed your teeth, then you can read a book with mom."

"It makes me happy when _____"

When talking about parenting phrases, remember that positive reinforcement is important when gaining cooperation and raising great listeners. Have you ever heard of the "Rubber Band Method?" This method involves keeping three rubber bands on your wrist and then each time you say something positive to your child, you move one rubber band to the opposite wrist. The goal is to say three encouraging and positive things to your kids at a minimum each day.

The "It makes me happy when _____" phrase is inspired by this idea. Try to use this phrase at least three times a day to encourage your kids. Kids desire our approval and positive affirmation. This phrase does exactly that. (See Chapter 12 for more encouraging phrases.)

"After you finish _____, we are going to _____"

If your child is fully engrossed with something and it is time to move on or leave, give them some advance warning to encourage an easier transition. Because toddlers and preschoolers do not fully understand the concept of time in minutes, hours, and days, it is better to use something different as a time barometer.

For example, "After you finish watching this TV show, we are going to eat dinner." Or "After you finish your puzzle, we are going to clean up the toys." Or "After we finish this book, you are going to bed."

Giving the completion of an activity as a time barometer for your child will help them transition more easily to the next task.

"Mmm...hmm."

Teaching kids to listen starts with listening as a parent. When your child speaks to you and says things like, "Mom, I didn't do it," or "He hit me," or the infamous "No!" go ahead and nod and smile and shower your child with a few "Mmm...hmms." This shows your child that you are actively listening. Your kids feel heard. They feel noticed. They feel validated. And when kids feel all those things, they demonstrate an increased propensity to listen.

"I'll know you're ready when _____"

This phrase comes in especially handy when kids are ignoring your directions. Kids move to the beat of their own clock and often take far longer to accomplish tasks than most parents would prefer. You may be the type of parent who wants everything done yesterday. (I'm raising my hand.) However, toddlers tend to see the journey as important as the destination. Preparing earlier and improving our own time management skills as parents and caregivers makes a huge difference.

You may ask your child to wash his hands for dinner, and he completely ignores what you are saying. A great parenting phrase to respond with would be, "I'll know you're ready for dinner when your hands are clean."

Teaching Kids to Listen Starts With Phrases

Whether your kids are throwing a tantrum in aisle six of Target, refusing to stay close in the parking lot, or standing naked on the counter to get a drink of water, your kids are hard-wired for empathy, listening, and obedience. Short listening phrases can help nurture and guide your child to build those skills. On days when everything feels like a power struggle or a temper tantrum, try one of these listening phrases and see how it works. Teaching kids to listen may not be so bad after all.

"Treat a child as though he already is the person he's capable of becoming."

Haim Ginott

Magical Mealtime Phrases

There we sat at the table. A family member had slaved away over a hot stove for quite a while, producing a beautiful and nutritious meal for the kids and me. I was excited to dig in, and as I picked up my spoon, I heard a tiny voice next to me say...

"This is yucky. I don't want to eat it."

I nearly fainted from shock. I hadn't heard that type of phrase come out of my child's mouth before. I addressed the phrase immediately and then set out to make our table a place of peace, not one of complaint.

While we aren't in control of our children's taste buds, preferences, and attitudes, we can encourage an attitude of gratefulness at the table. We don't have to get into dinnertime power struggles that make parents dread mealtime.

With a few key habits, helpful phrases, and even consequences when children step out of the boundaries, you'll find mealtimes transformed from a time of pickiness, stress, and confusion to one of harmony.

At least, as much peace and harmony as you can have with little ones.

"Taste before you waste"

Toddlers and preschoolers will often say they don't like something they haven't even tried. If it looks unfamiliar or doesn't resemble a treat, you may have a child who shoves their plate away before sampling. Some families require their children to take a set number of bites – or even to finish their whole plate –but this phrase is more general and can be adapted to your family rules.

Additionally, this gives you an opportunity to teach your children about the concept of waste. If you've lovingly prepared a meal no one will eat, the food bought and purchased with hard-earned money will go to waste. It will help teach children gratefulness and give them a better appreciation for the value of food.

"It's not over 'til it's over"

If your children are like mine, they want to jump down from the table the minute they are finished eating. If this occurs regularly, you might see your children eating less and less at mealtime and wanting to snack more.

By encouraging your children to remain at the table for a certain time period – whatever you think is reasonable – you're also teaching patience and self-control, which will aid them in many ways as they grow big and strong.

"Healthy food helps us grow strong"

Some of my children eat vegetables, no problem. Others tend to fight the green. However, they all realize which foods are healthy and which are not. This isn't to say we shouldn't treat our kids or have sugary sweets or ice cream on occasion, but it's important we teach our children the value of healthy food for their health and energy levels.

Not that small kids are low on energy...

When we see our children eating something that is nutrient dense, that is the perfect time to say, "Well done, healthy food helps us grow strong." In this scenario, you're affirming their choice to eat well. This is a positive praise that can help your child to be more willing to try the next healthy dish you offer.

"You get what you get and you don't pitch a fit"

We should strive to give our kids enough choices so they feel empowered. No mother wants to prepare meals for their family day in and day out that go uneaten. It's okay to offer a few healthy alternatives within a meal, but it's also important children realize that they need to act with respectful and thankful hearts for the meal provided to them.

This phrase is most effective as a general rule, not said in an angry voice if a child is initiating a power struggle. If your child understands they aren't to throw a tantrum over the dinner choice, they will begin learning how to manage their emotions and share their feelings without disrupting the entire meal.

"You have two choices: take it or leave it"

In our home, we're not fans of forcing our kids to eat their whole meal. In fact, we'll often ask they take one bite to taste, and if they don't want to eat it, let them make that choice. However, they do not get a second course or Plan B.

This phrase should be said kindly and in an effort to show your child they do have this choice. They are not forced to eat something they do not like. However, not liking dinner is not a way to get an entirely different meal prepared for them.

I've found this is difficult the first few times, but soon your children understand the family rules. At times, my kids will choose to forego dinner. The next morning, they'll wake up ready for a double portion of breakfast, and I'm okay with this too.

The goal is to offer your children nutrient dense healthy meals, not to have a child who is a slave to finishing their plate.

"A treat's not a treat if it's all we eat"

Do you have a sweet tooth? Did you pass it on to your kids?

Everyone loves a sweet (or savory) bite of something scrumptious. We can't help it! However, the danger comes when our children expect to eat more treats than regular meals. And particularly when they begin to resist the meals you've cooked but demand treats instead.

We are careful not to deprive children of sweets, but we tend to keep them out of eyesight. If the kids can't see the bag of tiny chocolate kisses in the pantry, they are less likely to ask for them. It's much harder to forget about a nice calorie rich snack if you see it every time you walk through the kitchen.

You can also give your children healthy snacks that taste like treats. I regularly make smoothies with bananas, strawberries, a few spinach leaves, and milk. To my kids, it's as good as ice cream, but I don't feel guilty.

"Thank the cook!"

My husband is adamant that the children learn to thank the person responsible for the meal. Our kids are not able to get down from the table and go play until they've thanked the cook. This is a great habit for a few reasons.

One, it teaches children to have a grateful heart. We know many people around the world don't have adequate food for survival, much less abundance. Our children, however, are not born with this information. It's important we teach our kids to be thankful for their provisions, and this will help prevent an attitude of entitlement towards food.

Second, it helps our young maturing children understand food does not appear from nothing. It must be bought (or grown), stored, prepared, then dished out. By involving kids in the entire food process in our homes, we help them to understand its importance and value.

And they are less likely to complain about food they are thankful for. Win, win!

After that fateful comment, we've worked hard to turn around our children's attitudes towards food. And our own as well. While mealtimes can still be stressful with small ones learning the ins and outs of eating, manners, and hand-eye-spoon coordination, our time at the table is much more enjoyable.

Yours can be too.

> *"Let her sleep. For when she wakes, she will move mountains."*

Attributed to Napoléon Bonaparte

Sleepy, Sleepy Time

I cringed every time I caught myself doing this. I was starting the kids' bedtime routine, and that's when the tantrums began. As soon as my son knew bedtime was starting, he weighed in with, "No sleep, no rest, no bath." This was his response to everything. The chant—no sleep, no rest, no bath—it was basically his life motto.

It's funny how when you put your kids to bed, they act like they've never slept before in their life. Kids act like sleep is poison.

In that moment, I felt so frustrated with all the "no sleep, no rest, no bath" chanting. My brain boiled to the brim with irritation. That's when the words exited my mouth, "If you don't want to take a bath, then you're going to bed right now. Do you want to go to bed right now?!"

I found myself doing this in other situations when my son didn't listen or obey:

"If you don't listen to mom, then you're going to bed right now."
"If you don't stop crying, then you have to take a nap. That's it! You're taking a nap."

This usually led us into a parent-child power struggle. Why is it that all a parent wants to do is sleep, and kids don't?

The Sleep Approach You're Missing

Sleep is a gift. Sleep is a treasure. As adults, you and I know this. All we want to do is finally get some sleep. To take a nap. To sleep all night and wake up to breakfast in bed – or at least coffee!

But here's the problem: I was treating sleep as a consequence to bad behavior. Sleep is not a consequence. Sleep is a gift, and without realizing it, I was inviting my child to fight bedtime by treating it as a consequence.

Helpful Phrases for an Easier Bedtime With Kids

Re-framing the idea of sleep can help kids see it in a positive light. Sleep heals our body. Sleep gives us energy. Sleep helps our brains learn new skills and process the day's events. It's the building block of child growth and development.

"Let's enjoy our cozy time together"

The goal is to help kids build a positive association with sleep. Sometimes bedtime can turn into one big chaotic mess. Turn it around and make it a cozy time. Turn the lights down, put on some gentle music, diffuse some essential oils, and turn bedtime into a relaxing spa routine – or as best you can!

A quick washing of the hands and face, followed by a nice lotion massage is one way to make cozy time simple yet inviting. Then invite your child to snuggle up on the couch and read for 10-15 minutes before bedtime. Did you know that 78 percent of kids say the reason they enjoy being read aloud to is that it's a special time with their parents?[3] Help make bedtime more enjoyable using the phrase, "Let's enjoy our cozy time together."

"You're going to feel so much better after you rest"

More than anything, we want our kids to learn and understand that sleep is here to help our bodies, not hurt us. Walk your child through a series of examples about how their body will feel better after a good night's rest.

"Did you know when you sleep, your brain grows bigger?"

Encourage your child to imagine their brain getting bigger and stronger each time it rests during the night. This is how kids learn to run faster, read books, jump higher, and recognize colors and shapes and numbers. Whatever

---

[3] Reading Aloud at Home. 2016. Scholastic Inc.

motivates your child, help them learn that their brain will grow bigger to help them accomplish something better and better each time.

An alternative yet similar phrase to use in this situation is, "Sleep helps your brain move all the things you learned today into the right spot." Encourage your child to imagine all the things they learned that day moving around in their brain like a giant puzzle putting itself together all throughout the night. You can even walk them through some guided imagery of this happening to help them relax before bedtime.

"Let's have a pajama race! Ready, set, go!"

As soon as you turn something into a game, you've connected at the child's level. Everything in life is a game to a child. Enjoy a pajama race, make silly monster faces while you brush teeth, and make up new and creative stories from the books you read.

An alternative phrase to use here is, "You found a way to make teeth brushing fun." Or "You found a way to make picking up the toys fun." This encourages your child to recognize their strengths during the bedtime routine and encourages cooperation rather than resistance.

"What dreams do you think you'll have tonight?"

Talking about dreams is a fun one. Kids come up with the wildest and most creative ideas. Ask about dreams and make up silly and fun things your child may dream about. Try to keep things light-hearted and fun.

If your kids aren't up for talking, see if they will draw you a picture of their dream. Drawing and coloring is a perfect calm activity to do right before bedtime. If your child is an older preschooler, he may even want to color while you read him a chapter book before bedtime. Kids can still understand and follow a story even when doodling or coloring a picture, as long as they aren't writing out numbers and letters.

This phrase is also useful if your child is struggling with nightmares. Talking about dreams can help your child process those thoughts and feelings. Additionally, kids can draw pictures of nightmares, tear them up, and throw them away as a symbolic gesture.

"Excuse me. I'll be right back."

This is the perfect phrase to use if your kids won't stay in bed during the night. The "excuse me" drill was developed by sleep behaviorist Dr. John Kuhn.

Here's how the "excuse me" phrase works:

On the first night, push bedtime back to a later time so your child is good and sleepy. Go through your normal bedtime routine and then lay your child down in his bed. Sitting next to him, offer comforting touches and after he is in bed for a bit say, "You're trying hard to stay in bed. Excuse me. I forgot something. I'll be right back."

Leave and come back a few minutes later. Resume touches and positive reinforcement such as, "You are snuggled up and relaxed so nicely in bed." Then leave again after you say, "You're doing a great job staying in bed. Excuse me. I need to go do something. I'll be right back." Continue repeating this at random intervals and slowly extending the amount of time you are out of the room before returning.

Ideas for excuses:

- I need to take out the garbage.
- I forgot to turn the light out.
- I have to go to the bathroom.
- I have an eyelash in my eye.
- I need to grab a tissue.

The goal: Allow your child to fall asleep when you are out of the room during an "excuse me" moment.

Each night, continue to increase the "excuse me" intervals, weaning your child from your presence in the room at bedtime. You can also use the "excuse me" technique during night waking to get your child to fall back asleep in their own bed.

Our New Bedtime

While shopping at the grocery store, I once heard a mom say, "These are the best parenting days of your life." I looked at her with a wary eye because the toddler and preschool years are hard, especially when bedtime battles are present.

But after nights of cozy and calming bedtime phrases, my son started patting the cushion of our couch three times each night as a signal it was time for me to sit for our "comfy time." Now, each night I follow his lead, snuggle up next to him and enjoy our time together.

Recently, he surprised me. One night before laying my son to sleep, I leaned in to give him one more kiss, and that's when he whispered something that made me know our new bedtime phrases were the right choice: "I sleep, mama. Night, mama."

Bedtime is something all parents struggle with at one point or another. These sleepy time phrases may not solve all your kids' bedtime and sleep problems, but they are a fresh and positive place to start.

"Never do for a child what he can do for himself."

Michelle LaRowe

Raising Independent Littles

I remember attempting to push a chair up to the sink. The chair was heavy for me, but I kept pushing, determined to get it over to the sink. After several minutes of pushing, the chair was exactly where I wanted it.

I was five years old.

I hopped up and stood on the chair proudly, looking at a sink full of dirty dishes. Now, this may surprise you, but I wanted to wash the dishes by hand. This was a rare moment. Because I'll be honest, the majority of the time, I wanted to play with Barbies and dress up. On this particular day, however, I wanted to do something special for my dad. The past week of work upset him, and even as a young girl, I remember it vividly.

So at age five, I pushed the chair up to the sink to start washing dishes. This was before we had a dishwasher. While I was busy washing, my dad was upstairs working in the home office; he had no idea what I was doing. About an hour later, he returned downstairs to find me standing at the sink playing with a doll next to a stack of mostly clean dishes.

I'll never forget the surprised look on his face when he walked into the kitchen. I felt so proud and independent in that moment, and the memory of that feeling is still burned inside me nearly 30 years later.

Now that I'm a parent myself, raising independent children is important to me. While I don't want my kids to be emotionally distant or independent from their family, I do want them capable and confident in their own abilities to handle life situations.

In the earliest years, your children count on you for nearly everything. As infants, they rely on you for food, bathing, comfort, play, and mobility. As your children grow, they become more independent in self-care but still depend on you for love, protection, guidance, and support. In the coming years, my goal is to help our kids achieve greater independence in all aspects of their lives in order to help them become healthy, thriving, and well-functioning adults in society.

Your kids don't have to know how to do everything to be confident and independent. They just have to feel confident enough to problem solve on their own and figure things out that are age and developmentally appropriate. Here are some phrases that will encourage your kids to become independent and capable little ones who grow into adults who are ready and willing to try new things.

"Just give it a try"

Certain personalities don't want to try anything they aren't already good at. If you've already explained enough that you know your child understands what needs to be done, let them give it a try. Stay close, but don't intervene before they've met and pushed through a little resistance.

"It's not that you can't, you just can't yet"

I get what people say when they do the whole "don't say 'I can't'" thing. But honestly, sometimes it's just the truth. If I say I can't speak Mandarin, that is a fact. So instead of arguing with kids about their current ability, look forward. "Let's give it a few tries, and then you'll get the hang of it. Sometimes we have to give a lot of effort before it works!" This is both a realistic and optimistic point of view.

"It doesn't matter how many tries it takes"

One thing I can't stand is when my kids quit before they've even started trying. There's wisdom in quitting something that's unwise, unfruitful, or wrong, but kids need to know that the majority of things in life take a lot of real hard work and effort. And that's okay.

"You can do it all by yourself"

I'm happy to help my kids do many things because I love them so much! However, with a lot of young kids, it's actually physically impossible to meet their constant requests. And even if it were possible, there's no sense in it. My 1-year-old can push a stool up to the sink, climb the stool, fill his cup with water, and drink it. And I let him. It sometimes makes a mess, but I will say I have found one thing: my kids love to do things on their own once given the opportunity.

"Why do you think that happened?"

It's not enough that we ask children to do things and expect them to cooperate. We actually need to teach them why things happen the way they do. Cause and effect. Chicken and the egg. The cart before the horse. After something goes one way or the other, it's wise to ask your children what they think about it. Get them involved in how things work. And honestly, the answers they give will be good fodder for their quote book.

"What do you think is the better choice?"

This works similarly to the question above because it gets kids involved. When I'm trying to get my children to do something and I am meeting a little resistance, I will often ask this question. Why this works well is because it lets you into their brain. Often you'll find out exactly why they are hesitating. As a Type-A mom, I tend to want things to happen quickly, but my daughter will often give me quite a lengthy explanation as to why she thinks what she does, and it helps me know her.

"What do you think is going to happen?"

Not only should you use this phrase when reading books to kids (because you really should), but this is simply a good way to get your children to actively engage in their life and what's going on. It requires them to think about the possible effects of their actions, and that's exactly the goal!

"You can help"

Whether you are working on a home project, cooking dinner, or encouraging your kids to get dressed, allowing them to actively participate along side you makes all the difference. The more hands-on experiences kids gain through cooking, cleaning, home projects, and self-care, the more independent they become. As a bonus when your kids are helping you, remember to remind them of their strengths, i.e. "You are a helper!" Sharing and verbalizing your child's strengths builds them up and encourages those strengths to grow and shine.

"You have choices"

It's perfect to name the specific choices for your kids in a given situation. "You have two choices: Do you want to wear the green striped shirt or the blue shirt today?" Ultimately, we want our kids to make good decisions in life independently of outside help, and this starts with offering the simplest choices from a young age and moving towards more complex choices as they get older. This teaches kids they have control over their lives, and it gives them the freedom to make their own independent decisions, priming them for independence.

"You're ready to do it alone"

Kids may try and try and try and not succeed in completing a task. But after the effort is there and your kids get the hang of it, encourage them to do something without any assistance at all. Buttoning pants, climbing up the rock wall at the playground, or getting a drink from the fridge are a few examples. Whichever tasks you would like your child to do independently, encourage them – when they are ready – to do it without assistance.

We Want Nothing But the Best for Our Children

We are always trying to help them succeed as best we can. It's hard not to swoop in and help them take their plate to the sink, put on their shoes, clean up their toys, or make their bed. This is how we express our love. We want to fix things and make life as easy as possible for our sweet babies. But in order to allow our kids to experience success in life, we have to allow them independence and a chance to problem solve without frequent outside help.

We have to sit back and hold our breath for a moment, even when it makes us cringe or we know that they will fail. We have to allow them to push the chair up to the sink, wash some dishes, and feel a moment of pride that they did it all by themselves. Even if three dishes broke, the washing was less than desirable, and Barbie hair is now on the dishes, the small steps you take to raise an independent child today will build them into a happy, healthy, and thriving adult down the road.

"If you want children to keep their feet on the ground, put some responsibility on their shoulders."

Abigail Van Buren

Cleaning, Chores, and Contribution

My daughter was 2 years old when I taught her to fold towels.

It didn't occur to me to wonder, "Is this an age appropriate chore?" Instead I asked myself, "What has to be done, and if shown how, can she do it?"

Turns out she could. And so could my sons. And now I'm out of the towel folding business. Which works out well for us since we use towels for bathing, sopping up spills, swimming, sitting, picnicking, and everything else under the sun.

My kids are Master Folders.

While we'd love to spend our days playing with the kids, family life involves more than having fun. Some tasks, chores, projects, and maintenance must be done for the home to run. If we want it to run smoothly, we have to do even more.

Servant-hearted mothers are often tempted to take on every To Be Done task in the home as a way to show their love to their family. While this is noble, it also robs our kids. Because working hard and seeing results feels good.

It teaches perseverance.
It teaches responsibility.
It teaches follow through.

And it's real life. In life, some things we have to do regardless of whether we "feel like it" or not. So having chores, contributions, and tasks we expect our children to carry out helps both the family as a unit and kids individually.

Plus, chores don't have to be so bad! With a bit of ingenuity and good systems in place, your family can maintain a tidy home without much fuss. In the meantime, here are some helpful phrases you can use to teach your children the value of work and responsibility.

As these phrases and others like them become part of your family vocabulary, you'll find children are not as resistant to helping out. In fact, once they realize what is expected of them, you may be surprised how quickly they get to work.

"We put things away, we don't put them down"

A great habit to get into is putting things away immediately after playing or using them. If children take out toys throughout the day but never clean up, the mess is so monumental it's difficult for older children to make a dent.

By encouraging kids to put things away they are using, you get less mess. When you see your child pull something out to use (or finish playing with a toy), encourage them to put it away immediately so you have less mess to clean up later.

"Work first, play later"

If you call out "chore time" and the kids don't come enthusiastically, this is a helpful phrase. Also, this phrase will help you remember about an effective order or routine. Instead of letting your children play a lot and then have chore time, why not start with chores?

It's harder to stop doing something fun and start doing something more tedious than it is to work hard quickly so you can move on to the fun stuff. Additionally, you get a built-in consequence for children who refuse to do their chores. No play!

"We all live here; we all help out"

A common phrase my kids will say is, "But I didn't make this mess!" While each child does normally clean up after themselves, occasionally the house is a mess because we all live in it. I've been known to tell the children that I don't make most of the messes in the house, but I still clean up.

When your little ones begin to grumble or complain they don't like cleaning or helping outside, this phrase is a great reminder that everyone in the family needs to pull their weight for things to run smoothly.

"Come get me when it's done"

A common mistake we moms often make is asking our children to do something, but forgetting to check that it's done properly. No, we shouldn't let our OCD tendencies redo all of our children's hard work, but we also need to make sure our little ones have understood our instructions.

Checking our little ones' work does a few things. First, it keeps them accountable to finish. Second, it helps inspire them to work fast since they don't get to move on to the next thing until the first is finished. Third, it helps keep them on task. If our preschooler was doing a 5-minute job and hasn't been seen for 15 minutes, we know to go looking.

"The fun's not over until it's put away"

One of the biggest reasons our homes turn untidy quickly is because of toys. While we'd never begrudge our children their toys (most of them, anyway) the situation can get out of hand easily. Decluttering and downsizing have their place, but if your children learn to pick up after themselves from a young age you won't have to threaten them with Toy Armageddon.

Any time your children have a concentrated period of play with their toys, teach them to put it away before moving on. Playtime then screen time? Put the toys away before the TV comes on. Toy time before lunch? Put the toys away before coming to the table. Toy time after nap? Put the toys away before getting ready for dinner. And on and on.

When this becomes an everyday part of your children's routine, you'll be amazed how many power battles you avoid.

Let's Be Real: Chores Aren't Always Fun

Even using these helpful phrases, you'll still have days when things don't go to plan. The kids fight cleaning. You fight picking up, and you wonder if they'll ever learn to be responsible kids who contribute to the running of the home.

But they will.
Towel by towel.
Toy by toy.

The habits we build now will bear fruit sooner than you think, and before you know it, your little ones will be active participants in the running of the household.

"You're off to great places! Today is your day! Your mountain is waiting, so...get on your way!"

Dr. Seuss

Public Places, Strangers, and New Situations

We were at the Sydney Harbour Bridge on a nice family walk. I was strolling slowly, waddling my pregnant belly around with care. My husband pushed one child and another two walked beside us. They were small and didn't want to stray too far from us.

Then, all of a sudden...WHOOSH. Right beside us, a boy slightly older than my kids blew by us in a hurry on the run. We all stopped and watched him for a bit as he tore off ahead. Then from behind I heard, "Ethan, stop right now!"

He turned his head, obviously having heard her request, then kept running at full speed. He was going further and further away from her, and she was unable to keep up. In fact, she had to stop running and bend over to catch her breath.

He wasn't slowing down, she wasn't catching up, and it was not a good situation. Large crowds surrounded them, and I could sense her panic growing.

Finally someone yelled, "Boy, go back to your mom now!"

And you know what? He did.

Who's to say his reasons for running, but the situation taught me one thing that day. We need clear rules with our kids in uncertain situations. In public places. When crowds are around. We can't expect them to understand why we're scared or what they should not do.

We've Got to Tell Them And Repeat It Frequently

"It's okay to feel nervous"

Children often think the fact that they feel nervous means something is wrong. Or they shouldn't do something, try something, or continue forward. We adults know different. By using a statement that has no shame or stigma attached like "it's okay to feel nervous," we're communicating that our child's feelings are perfectly valid.

"It's okay to feel nervous, but we have to go inside and see the doctor," is much better than saying, "I know you feel scared, but we're doing it anyway." Often children simply want their feelings validated, and that alone gives them the courage to face the new challenge.

"Hand on tire"

If you have multiple children, you know the struggle that is Parking Lots. You can't hold every kid in your arms, but you need them to stay close by. We have a "hand on tire" rule in our family. Of course, you can easily do "hand on side of van" if you're worried about tire germs.

The rule goes like this: when your child gets out of the vehicle they are not allowed to walk anywhere in the parking lot but must put their hand on the tire and wait until you're ready to walk together. If you have to unbuckle a baby or put him in a carrier or stroller, you'll appreciate your slightly older children using their self-control and patience to wait until you're ready to make the move across the lot as one family.

This is a great habit to get into if you have a child who is tempted to wander or run.

"Can you see me?"

Kids should never wander out of our eyesight. Particularly in public spaces, busy areas, or when we are the only adult with them. Some children are more prone to wander than others, but it's a good idea to teach this phrase from a young age.

I don't know about you, but my kids like to run ahead in the grocery store and turn corners without me. "Can you see me?" is a question I'll ask as they begin their advance. That's a good reminder to them they are not allowed to go far from me.

Some scenarios are clearly safer than others, but by using this as a general rule, your kids will have a point of reference. At a birthday party, family reunion, or even church event, asking your kids to stay within view of you helps them to explore and have fun while you are able to keep a close eye on them.

"A 'hello' will do"

Some adults may ask your children for a hug or kiss. Most parents now agree requiring children to show physical affection is not a good idea. It sends mixed signals to the child that they are not in charge of their own body and choices. We want our kids to know they are able to refuse a hug, kiss, or advance if they are uncomfortable.

However, this can get awkward, right? A family member demands a hug, and your child hides behind your leg. Now suddenly, the adult expects you to make the kiss go forward. There's a better way! If you sense your child is nervous to greet another person, use the phrase, "A 'hello' will do."

This communicates to the other person you aren't forcing your child to hug but also shows your child you expect them to greet the adult politely. A simple "hello" will work just fine. This lets your child know they are expected to be polite but not expected to give affection when they are uncomfortable.

"I'm a step away"

I have one child who does not like new things. Unless the "thing" is a toy and then that's okay. A new situation? New expectation? New responsibility? No, not very much. I used to present the job or task and give him space to complete it.

That really didn't work well.

Not that he wasn't capable, but something about my presence reassures him, even if I'm not actively helping. So now, when I ask him to do or try something new, I stand with him. "I'm a step away" communicates this.

"I know it's tricky, but I'm a step away"

"This really makes you nervous, huh? Thank goodness I'm a step away!"

Sometimes the child doesn't want you to take over – just to be a supportive bystander. Even adults like to feel supported. Children are no different!

"It's hard until it's not"

My son is reluctant to try new things. His siblings can run with wild abandon into a new setting, and he stays back, worried it'll be hard. That he can't do it well. That he'll look silly. That it'll be too much work. He thinks things should be easy or that we should avoid them.

Hey, sometimes I can't blame him.

We've made great headway with him by teaching him that it's okay when things are hard. "Yes, right now you don't know how to do it, so it'll be hard...until it's not." I am often heard saying this type of phrase when he's attempting a new chore or job.

"It's hard. Some things are just not easy at first. It'll be hard until it's not."

Often this is enough encouragement for him to feel that he is not inadequate or incapable, he simply has to keep trying.

"You stay by me, I stay by you"

My daughter used to be nervous in social situations. Not social anxiety per se but a reluctance to enter into the fray. Some children are born social butterflies with little inhibition or shyness. Others struggle feeling comfortable in situations that are overwhelming.

If you're taking your child to a big event, party, or place where they are likely to feel overwhelmed, a good rule of thumb is to get down to their eye level, hold their little hands or put your arms around them and tell them, "You stay by me, I stay by you."

Though they are little and not analyzing the nuances of your words, this phase communicates two things: first that they are responsible to stay by you and second that you are going to stay by them.

Children are going to get nervous, get overwhelmed, and need guidance in new and different situations. It's important as parents we are very clear about our boundaries, expectations, and consequences.

Children thrive knowing what to expect.

Children thrive knowing you are in control.

Children feel brave when they know you are right there with them.

"You are braver than you believe, stronger than you seem, and smarter than you think."

Winnie the Pooh

A "Phrase" of Encouragement

When I was a little girl growing up in the Midwest, my dad and I spent most evenings playing Trivial Pursuit for Kids at the kitchen table. Each night, I desperately wanted to fill my colored trivial pursuit pie before my dad. I wanted to win. While the trivia questions in the kids' version were far easier than the adult version, they were still hard. Especially for a 7-year-old.

Night after night, I would lose in Trivial Pursuit, and my dad would win. Of course he won. He knew far more answers to the trivia questions as an adult than I did as a 7-year-old child. But my dad never let me win.

I lost.

I lost.

I lost again.

I cried each time I lost. It was frustrating and upsetting to lose again and again each night. I experienced struggle, disappointment, and failure. Yet each night, he encouraged me to persevere through the game using a series of helpful phrases. Now years later, as a parent myself, I use many of these exact phrases with my kids, plus a few more for good measure.

The Right Kind of Encouragement Is Important

The phrases we choose to use when encouraging our kids makes a huge difference, and research support this. But first, I know the praise you use – regardless of the type – comes from a place of love. You want your kids to know you've got their backs. You want them to know you love them unconditionally. That no matter what, you think they are amazing, smart, and worthy. However, it's important to know that while children thrive on praise, we must choose the right type of praise.

Using the phrases "Good job" or "You won" or "You're so smart" provides a momentary good feeling due to positive attention, but it does not give any clue as to why it is a "good job" or a "win" or "smart."

Research shows that regularly saying a generic phrase like "Good girl" or "Way to go" each time your child masters a skill makes her dependent on your affirmation rather than her own motivation.

Over time, kids view themselves as good or bad, and they will start to seek out small and trivial tasks to earn the praise of "good job" and get as many "quick wins" as possible. In doing so, kids are more inclined to develop both narcissism and entitlement.

We know from research[4] that, "When children are seen by their parents as being more special and more entitled than other children, they may internalize the view that they are superior individuals, a view that is at the core of narcissism. However, when children are treated by their parents with affection and appreciation, they may internalize the view that they are valuable individuals, a view that is at the core of self-esteem."

What Types of Praise Are Most Helpful?

Using phrases that directly comment on or describe what the child is doing well are considered most useful when filling your child's self-esteem tank and reinforcing positive behavior. For example, "I see you are working hard to build that tower." Or "I noticed you were trying hard to use your manners at dinner. I really appreciate that." Or "I can tell you are making an effort to share with your sister."

All of the above example phrases describe something specific that a child did well using effort, hard work, and problem-solving skills appropriate for his or her age and development.

While the list of phrases below is not specific to things a child did well, they are encouraging children towards effort rather than the result, which is the ultimate goal of using phrases to encourage problem solving, perseverance, and tenacity.

---

[4] Brummelman, E. 2014. Origins of Narcissim in Children. *PNAS.* 112(12). 3659-3662.

This extensive list of phrases is self-explanatory. We hope this list offers you a generous number of ideas and inspires you to develop some of your own.

I can see you're really trying!
Keep on trying!
You almost got it!
I can see you tried hard.
I'm proud of you for trying.
I appreciate your help.
How do you feel about that?
I'm glad you enjoy learning!
I'll bet you knew you could do it!
You make my job easy.
You're really giving that your best!
You're the bright spot in my day.
What you have to say matters.
You've just about got it.
You're really improving.
You're getting better!
I can see you want to get it just right.
Now you have it.
Now you've figured it out!
That's really creative.
Thanks for helping make this a good day!
Nice going!
That's the way to do it.
I'm listening.
You did it that time!
One more time, and you'll have it!
Look how far you've come!
Hey, you did it!
Wow!
I believe in you.

I believe you.
I trust you.
I'm so happy for you.
You must feel pretty proud!
You're really going to town.
You must feel happy about that.
You've made a lot of progress.
That's a tough one, but I'll be you can figure it out.
You are honest.
I like the way you handled that!
You remembered.
You're fun to be around.
You make me a better person.
You must've been practicing.
Your opinions matter.
I accept who you are.
You're making a difference.
I love spending time with you.
You make my heart full.
I love you.
You can try again tomorrow.
That was a responsible choice.
You used your imagination.
You were a real help today.
You are kind and thoughtful.
You really worked hard on that.
I appreciate your help.
Give yourself a pat on the back!
I love watching you play.
I love seeing the world your way.
I appreciate you.
You are thinking through your choices.
You did a lot of work today!
Look how far you've come!

You calmed yourself.
That took a lot of courage.
You set a positive example for others.
You are dedicated.
You're improving!
You're really getting that hang of it.
I think you can do it.
I have a nice time when you are along.
Being with you is a treat for me!
You made it!
You did it all by yourself.

The Positive Outcomes of Praising for Effort

When you encourage your child using phrases that focus on effort rather than results, you are doing three very important things:

You cultivate perseverance.
You cultivate tenacity.
You cultivate hope.

You teach your child to persist despite difficulty or delay in success, even if takes days, months, or years to succeed. You teach your child that not reaching a goal does not equal the end. They learn to wake up again in the morning and try again. And you teach your child that you always have hope to do better.

When I think back to summer nights playing Trivial Pursuit with my dad, I realize a few things. It would've been easier for him to let me win. To avoid the tears. To avoid seeing me struggle. To say "Good job" and call it a day.

Sometimes praising our kids in a way that is most useful to them doesn't come easy. Old habits are hard to break. But laying the groundwork will make all the difference and help turn your child into the hard-working problem-solver every parent wants.

"The children who need the most love will ask for it in the most unloving ways."

Russell Barkley

Phrases to Avoid or Minimize

I took my son to story time at the library so we could get out of the house, mainly so I could talk to other adults and socialize, even it was only for 30 minutes. Each day at story time for about 15 minutes, the kids are allowed to play together. My son was struggling with a major biting issue at the time, and I was watching him like an Alaskan hunter with eyes on a moose.

I'm Going to Confess Something to You

From the time my son was 12 months old until he reached age 24 months, it's conservative to estimate he bit nearly fifty other children. Yes. Fifty. It brings tears to my eyes sharing that with you right now because that is an insane number of children to bite. And because working through a year of biting is an insanely long time.

While I was intently watching my son play in the children's room at the library, another mom walked up to me and asked, "How are you doing?" I shared about how we planned on visiting the aquarium on Saturday and my crockpot recipe for dinner that night. The Alaskan hunter in me was still watching my moose out of the corner of my eye. That's when I noticed some questionable movement. Whipping my head to the right, I saw it happen in slow motion: my son tackled another kid and bit him in the face before I could whisk him away.

I felt more like a parenting failure in that moment more than any other since I became a mom. As the other moms stared at me, the weight of the walls seemed to come down on my shoulders. From that moment forward, I removed my son from nearly all social situations so that he wouldn't bite or hurt other kids until we could resolve his behavior.

It was a lonely and challenging time for me as a mom. I felt like I was doing it all wrong. I felt like a failure as a parent. This is an important story because I want you to know I'm not a perfect parent. I make mistakes, fall down, learn, and pick myself back up.

I've also made my fair share of parenting mistakes when it comes to phrases. On the really tough days, even I catch myself saying the phrases in this chapter that are typically best to avoid in parenting.

From time to time, you may catch yourself using these phrases too. Remember that your child won't end up in therapy and ruined for life. And everything will come out just fine.

Phrases to Avoid Or Minimize With Kids

In most situations, these phrases are best avoided because they instigate power struggles, decrease self-esteem, and discourage listening.

"No...Don't"

I'm not suggesting that you remove all the "don't" or "no" commands from your communication, but making a shift towards minimizing them helps you become more effective as a parent. Using "no" and "don't" phrases can desensitize kids to their meaning, and they also require kids to process two pieces of information at the same time:

"What doesn't she want me to do?" and "What does she want me to do instead?"

This is confusing, especially for young kids, which is why you may find kids don't listen very well to these types of commands.

"No" and "don't" commands also reinforce negative behavior. Instead of hearing what you want her to do, your child is reminded of what she shouldn't do. When you say, "Don't stand on the chair," your child hears "stand on the chair." Cognitively, this is how children interpret phrases like that.

Lastly, kids find these types of phrases very discouraging. Imagine if 90 percent of the feedback you received at your job during the day was negative. It's incredibly defeating, and you may feel tempted to throw your hands up in the air and walk out the door. You may also think about picking a fight at the office to push back and show your boss that he can't walk all over you. This is exactly how kids feel.

The solution: save "no" and "don't" phrases for situations when you need a swift response, like stopping your child before he runs into a busy street or before he bites someone. This will cultivate better listening and cooperation in the long run.

"How many times have I told you?"

Using this phrase immediately puts kids on the defensive. The message you want to send to your kids is best shared as clear and concise messaging. Instead, say exactly what you are feeling in the moment. "I'm upset because I need to tell you the same thing many times." Or "I feel frustrated when I need to repeat myself." That is ultimately the message you want to share with your child and they are more like to respond cooperatively and make changes when they understand the root of the problem.

"Because I said so"

So many times throughout the day, you feel exhausted as a parent. The redundancy and constant guidance of your kids makes you weary. But saying, "Because I said so" doesn't give the child constructive feedback on why they can't do a certain something, nor does it offer them something to do instead. If you have a reason your child cannot do or say something, share it with them. It's the perfect opportunity for a teachable moment.

"I'm going to count to three"

Counting to three implies that you do not mean it the first time, and it encourages your kids to wait to listen until you count to three. Set your boundary the first time, stick to it, and move forward with your day. You don't need to count to three or offer multiple chances in most situations, especially if your child is already familiar with what is expected. After setting the boundary the first time, they will start to remember.

"Don't make me..."

As much as parents like to blame kids by saying "don't make me pull the car over" or "get up from this chair" or "yell at you," the truth is kids aren't making you doing anything. You are choosing to take a specific action, and the best action to take is to say exactly what you mean, rather than waste your energy on threats that don't work very well. You may opt to try, "If you don't stop hitting your brother, I will stop the car. The consequence will be..."

The same goes for "You're making me so mad." It's easy to fall into a trap and blame others for our emotions. Your child doesn't make you mad. His actions do. Say to your child exactly what is happening or what you are feeling. "I am mad when you don't pick up your toys."

This simple communication helps your child connect the message to an actual problem, rather than leaving them to guess. As your kids start to mature, the problem-solving wheels in the brain – the synapses – will start turning when presented with a challenge or problem that needs a solution.

"Stop crying, or I'll give you something to cry about"

When a child (or anyone for that matter) expresses a feeling, that feeling is real to him, even if you cannot understand why he is feeling that way or if the feelings seem trivial to you. When adults say things like, "You're fine," "Don't worry," "Stop whining," "Stop crying," or "Big boys / girls don't cry," you are invalidating your child's feelings.

Research finds that children whose feelings are repeatedly invalidated learn not to trust themselves. It is very confusing for them. If a child feels frustrated and begins to cry but then her mother, whom she looks to as an authority figure, tells her that she's okay, she becomes confused. Whom should she believe, her mother or herself? Research shows that this breaks down your child's self-esteem.

Instead, encourage your kids to get it all out and validate their emotions. "You're really sad / angry / upset right now because…" You can still hold the firm boundary you set while voicing and validating your child's emotions.

"Wait until your dad (or mom) gets home"

Kids often view this phrase as a threat, which usually becomes an empty threat because the follow-through is lacking. It's also watered-down discipline. To gain the most cooperation, it is best for parents and caregivers to take care of a situation immediately. This helps kids build the strongest connection between behavior and consequences. Don't allow your teachable moment to get lost in the time delay or invalidate your authoritativeness as a parent.

"Why can't you be more like your sister?"

Kids develop at different rates and each has their own unique temperament and personality. Comparing your child to someone else says, "I wish you were different, and I would like you more if you were like someone else." Children are impressionable little people, and these phrases stick with them throughout the years. And as much as we hope comparison will change behavior, this tactic does not motivate kids in any capacity.

In fact, it breaks down their self-esteem and causes them to feel defeated and do the exact opposite. Your child may think, "I'm never going to be like my sister, so I'm not going to try at all." Instead, encourage your child's strengths: "Wow, you put the toys away all by yourself!" Or "Thank you for listening."

Change Is Hard, But Change Is Growth

Whatever phrases you use in your home, know this: do what works for you and your family. There are no right or wrong phrases to use but rather phrases to use more often and phrases to use less. By avoiding the phrases shared in this chapter, you will start to see fewer power struggles, fewer tantrums, and better cooperation. It's time to enjoy better days with your kids.

Conclusion

Several years ago, I took a trip back to the Midwest to reconnect and visit with family while my husband was away at training. Exhausted from the day, I literally melted into a plush black leather recliner at 9 p.m. with my laptop propped on my legs. My oldest (still a baby at the time) was fast asleep, and it was a chance for me to enjoy some quiet.

That's where I spent several hours perusing mom blogs, looking to discover a connection with another mom – out there – somewhere. I wasn't a blogger yet nor an author. I was simply a new mom trying to find her way in the vast sea of parenting advice, tips, and ideas. The waves of opinions crashed over me as I tried to come up for air.

To be honest, I had no idea what I was doing in motherhood. I felt like I was drowning. Things didn't exactly go as "planned" when I first became a mom. My son was colicky, I was hormonal, and my husband and I experienced some growing pains in our marriage. All normal things yet completely overwhelming at the time.

It was that night that I discovered Rachel and her blog A Mother Far From Home. I read post after post, and after each one, I felt as if she was sitting right next to me like a best friend at a coffee shop.

I never dreamed that night would become the start of a very close friendship. And I certainly never thought we would spend the next several years blogging together, writing books together, commiserating over the tough days of motherhood together, and of course, sharing our biggest parenting victories together.

Over the past several years, Rachel and I have learned one thing: parenting is like a hurricane raging in the Pacific.

It's overwhelming and powerful, and it can tear down your house. The toddler and preschool years are no exception, and many – if not most – parenting days wash your patience and energy out from under you.

Helpful Phrases is a simple yet effective tool all parents can use when parenting feels like a raging storm. When your kids won't listen, they act like they are in charge, or they insist on throwing a tantrum in public, remember *Helpful Phrases*. When your kids are struggling at bedtime, at the dinner table or with cleaning and contribution, remember *Helpful Phrases*. And when your kids need encouragement or a push for independence or you don't know how to respond, remember *Helpful Phrases*.

In many ways, I feel like Rachel and I were sitting down having a cup of coffee with you throughout this book Helpful Phrases. We spent the last few hours shooting the parenting breeze on your comfy couch. Rachel has a Diet Coke because she's weird like that. I have black coffee because I'm even weirder. You have your favorite drink too, and no matter how weird it is, we like you anyway. Even when we all choose a different drink, we all have something in common: the desire to use practical and common sense parenting phrases to make everyday life with kids easier on ourselves.

Bonus Chapter: Encouraging Structured Playtime

Ready for your day to start running even smoother? Structured playtimes are the perfect way to help children learn exactly how to play well throughout the day, minimizing the need for nagging, yelling, and reminding.

As children learn what to expect and master routines themselves, they feel more confident and tend to follow along with the playtime routines without much instruction.

Starting Playtime Routines

Independent play occurs when a child plays alone without any siblings – usually in an area of the house with a physical boundary. This may be the crib, playpen, or bedroom depending on their age.

Structured playtime is a period of time when your child will complete a certain activity. This needn't be anything complicated, but it is a time that a child completes an activity with an objective. This may be painting, coloring, flashcards, art activities, learning activities, or reading time with you. Depending on your child's age, structured playtime may be an individual activity but will most often occur with an adult.

Free play is a time when your child plays free with no agenda. He may go from room to room or go outside, or he may do anything of his choosing that is within usual guidelines.

Family time generally occurs in the evenings when every family member is home. This may be dinner, couch time after dinner, daily devotionals, walks, or anything in between. It's generally a time where everyone makes an effort to be together.

It's easy to get creative with playtime routines throughout the day. A basic way to start is to simply have some sort of structured playtime at the same time each day. This may mean one of the following:

Your children play independently in separate rooms at the same time each morning.

Your children play together at the same time each afternoon.

You all enjoy family playtime each evening right after dinner.

Regardless of the playtime routines you incorporate into your daily life, structured playtime that is the same each day can help keep everyone accountable when it comes to making quality time for each other.

You will notice that sometimes, we encourage the use of a timer. This isn't meant to be stringent or rigid in nature. Sometimes the timer is helpful for children to understand that structured playtime ends when the timer goes off rather than after only five minutes. The goal is to help everyone (especially during family time) to commit to playing together for a set amount of time.

The timer is completely optional, and if you find your family does perfectly well without a timer, then by all means skip it. It is often just as easy to keep an approximate mental timer yourself and let the kids know when it's time to move on to something else.

Sample 1

This is a simple routine you can use to help your child play independently each day. If you are just getting started, you may want to start with as short as 5 to 15 minutes and work your way up to an age-appropriate amount of time.

1. Create a kid-safe play area (playpen or room)
2. Help your child choose toys to play with
3. Set the timer
4. Allow child to play for a set amount of time independently
5. Timer goes off
6. Offer appreciation or praise for playing well

Sample 2

To encourage children to play well together during a structured activity, incorporate this simple routine into your day. The structured activity may even be as simple as having the kids choose several toys to play with together. Or if desired, it could be a game, craft, or activity they choose together or that you create for them.

Create a game or structured activity for kids to focus on
Encourage kids to problem solve and play well together
Set the timer or simply set a mental 1-hour time limit
Allow kids to work through the activity
Playtime ends
Offer appreciation or praise for playing well

Sample 3

This is a favorite routine of ours because it encourages us to commit to family time each and every day. It's all too easy to get caught up in electronic devices and forget that interacting and playing together as a family is so important.

1. Turn all electronic devices off and put away
2. Create a game or activity to do as a family
3. Set the timer or set a mental time limit
4. Work together and enjoy the time
5. Family time ends

Offer appreciation or praise for quality time together and everyone does something of their choosing

If you are looking to incorporate a little more structure, and a little less chaos into your days, give structured playtime and independent playtime a try.

For a step-by-step guide on incorporating routines into your family life, view our book Routines, Rhythms and Schedules: How to Simplify Life with Kids.

http://www.themilitarywifeandmom.com/routines-rhythms-schedules-book

Bonus Chapter: Discovering a Routine That Works for Your Family

The benefits of a routine are undeniable. You know what to expect. The kids know what to expect, and daily life runs more smoothly. Whether you are more structured or embrace unscheduled time, you can still enjoy a daily routine or rhythm that can transform your home from one of chaos to one of calm.

What's a Routine?

Routine can mean:

Regularity and consistency within your day
A series of "one thing happens before another" actions
Using the clock as a guide (whether general or specific) for the day's activities

Routine need not mean:

Letting the clock be your master
Always doing the same things every day

Throwing spontaneity out the window

The major events of the day make up the foundation of the routine. For little ones, this includes sleep, eating, and play. From infants to preschoolers, these still remain the most important activities. If you are creating a routine from scratch, start with times of your choosing for the basics, then add in all the extras.

Benefits of a Routine

The benefits of routine are widely documented and accepted. In fact, many successful business people and entrepreneurs will go so far as to say that eating the same exact thing every morning for breakfast is part of their routine. Why? They want to save all their decision-making bandwidth for more important daily tasks. While we don't need to be that rigid, this example serves as a reminder that a routine can allow us to save much of our energy for the important things.

Routines are beneficial for children because they:

Give a sense of security and stability
Help develop self-discipline
Eliminate power battles
Breed cooperation (children like to do what's next when they know what it is)
Help the family find a good sleep rhythm

For a step-by-step guide on incorporating routines into your family life, view our book Routines, Rhythms and Schedules: How to Simplify Life with Kids.

http://www.themilitarywifeandmom.com/routines-rhythms-schedules-book

Resources and References

Websites

A Mother Far From Home by Rachel Norman – No-nonsense thoughts for loving and nurturing moms. From physical, mental, and emotional aspects of motherhood to household tips, I tell it like it is and like I pray it will be.

http://amotherfarfromhome.com/

The Military Wife and Mom by Lauren Tamm – Around here, I write about practical parenting, enjoying motherhood, and navigating the ups and downs of military life.

http://www.themilitarywifeandmom.com/

Books

Routines, Rhythms and Schedules: How to Simplify Life with Kids.

http://www.themilitarywifeandmom.com/routines-rhythms-schedules-book

For the Love of Sleep: Practical Baby Sleep Solutions for the Everyday Mama

http://www.themilitarywifeandmom.com/sleep

Lies That Make You Pay & Truths That Set You Free: A Mother's Guide to the Simple and Frugal Life

http://amotherfarfromhome.com/lies-that-make-you-pay-truths-that-set-you-free-a-mothers-guide-to-the-simple-frugal-life/

Can the Kids Come Too?

http://amotherfarfromhome.com/traveling-with-kids/

Printables

To download the 12 printables included with the book, please visit the URL:

http://www.themilitarywifeandmom.com/helpful-phrases-printables/

Use the password: PHRASES12

Please note, the password is case sensitive and contains no spaces.

48540782R00074

Made in the USA
Columbia, SC
09 January 2019